MW00907565

Daniel Fast Smoothies

Scrumptious and Nutritious Blend of Flavors That Make Up a Mouth Watering Array of Smoothie Beverages

Disclaimer

Contents

What You Will Find In This Book?

Everyone loves to wake up in the morning and be greeted by a refreshing smoothie. Quick and easy to make smoothies come with their own tag line of bearing colors and natural flavors.

But nobody wants to drink the same beverage again and again all the time. The **50 Daniel Fast Smoothie Recipes** caters to the long search of the best smoothie beverage recipe collection.

If you are a working mother or a busy bee, you can still enjoy the healthy benefits and the refreshing taste of a freshly made smoothie, with this month's worth of smoothie menu for breakfast or a healthy snack.

The **50 Daniel Fast Smoothie Recipes** recipe book includes:

1. Healthy and easy to make Daniel Fast approved smoothie recipes.

2. A Range of various Smoothies for Breakfast.

3. Beverage recipes with solely fruit ingredients.

4. Smoothies with creative and rich in flavor ingredients.

5. Preparation time, serving size and nutritional facts along with every recipe.

With this book you won't even need to skim through the beverage section of recipe pages, looking for a way to make a fruity and natural drink. Just flip the page and read on for the nutritious list of time saving and healthy smoothie recipes.

Refreshing Smoothies for Lunch

Blueberry and Vanilla Smoothie

Serves 2
Nutritional Value: Calories: 282, Total Carbohydrates: 25g, Total Fats: 11g, Protein: 9g

Prep Time: 5 minutes (prepare ingredients overnight)

Ingredients
1 Oz chia seeds
1 Oz vanilla protein powder
2 teaspoon pure vanilla extract
2 Oz oats
1 Cup frozen blueberries
3 cups almond milk

Instructions
Save the blueberries and shake the rest of the ingredients in a glass jar or container and freeze over night. In the morning, toss all ingredients into the blender and blend until smooth.

Black Berry Smoothie

Serves 2

Nutritional Value: Calories: 734, Total Carbohydrates: 21.1g, Total Fats: 63.4g, Protein: 29.6g

Prep Time: 5 minutes

Ingredients

1 Oz chia
2 cups almond milk
2 cups black berries
2 scoops vanilla whey protein powder

Instructions

Pour ingredients in blender and blend for around 45 seconds or until completely smooth.

Strawberry Smoothie with Cashew Sprinkles

Serves 2
Nutritional Value: Calories: 399, Total Carbohydrates: 57.1g, Total Fats: 12.2g, Protein: 17.0g

Prep Time: 5 minutes

Ingredients

2 cup strawberries
Dash of stevia
1 teaspoon vanilla
2 teaspoon lemon juice
2 teaspoon apple cider vinegar
1 Oz cashews
1 Oz chia seed
3 Oz oats
2 cups non diary milk

Instructions

Save the cashews and mix the rest of the ingredients in a jar to freeze overnight. In the morning, blend all the frozen ingredients until smooth. Sprinkle cashews on top of the smoothie before serving.

Strawberry Smoothie with Cashew Sprinkles

Apple and Cherry Smoothie

Serves 1

Nutritional Value: Calories: 434, Total Carbohydrates: 51.8g, Total Fats: 19.7g, Protein: 14.2g

Prep Time: 5 minutes

Ingredients

¼ cup fresh cherries
6 ice cubes
¼ cup water
2 teaspoons chia seeds
¼ cup fresh raspberries
½ of an apple
¼ English cucumber

Instructions

Pick out the cherry seeds and place all the ingredients into the blender. Blend until smooth.

Lemon Smoothie

Serves 2
Nutritional Value: Calories: 505, Total Carbohydrates: 54.5g, Total Fats: 24.4g, Protein: 23.3g

Prep Time: 5 minutes (prepare ingredients overnight)

Ingredients
Dash of white stevia
Zest of 2 lemons
2 teaspoon pure vanilla extract
3 teaspoons poppy seeds
1 Oz chia seeds
1 Oz almond butter
1 Oz lemon juice
2 Oz rolled oats
1 cup raspberries
3 cups non diary milk

Instructions
Pour all ingredients in a jar or any other container and freeze overnight. In the morning put all the jars contents in the blender and blend until smooth.

Chia Smoothie

Serves 2

Nutritional Value: Calories: 274, Total Carbohydrates: 28.2g, Total Fats: 7.0g, Protein: 25.2g

Prep Time: 5 minutes (prepare ingredients overnight)

Ingredients

1 Oz chia seeds
2 scoops protein powder
2 cups green tea
12 strawberries
1 banana

Instructions

Place all ingredients in a jar and store in the fridge over night (this will allow the chia to turn gelatinous). IN the morning toss the ingredients in the blender and blend until smooth.

Pumpkin and Maple Smoothie

Serves 2
Nutritional Value: Calories: 233, Total Carbohydrates: 28.2g, Total Fats: 5.5g, Protein: 10.0g

Prep Time: 5 minutes

Ingredients
Dash of all spice
½ teaspoon ground cloves
½ teaspoon crushed nutmeg
¼ teaspoon crushed ginger
½ teaspoon crushed cinnamon
1 teaspoon pure vanilla extract
1 teaspoon maple syrup
1 banana
1 cup canned pumpkin
2 cups non diary milk

Instructions
Toss all the ingredients into the blender and blend till they are smooth (around 30 to 45 seconds)

Cacao and Butter Smoothie

Serves 2

Nutritional Value: Calories: 805, Total Carbohydrates: 79.2g, Total Fats: 49.8g, Protein: 22.9g

Prep Time: 5 minutes (prepare ingredients overnight)

Ingredients
½ teaspoon vanilla extract (pure)
1 Oz cacao powder
1 Oz almond butter
1 Oz chia seeds
6 Oz oats
1 cup almond milk (unsweetened)

Instructions
Save half of the almond milk and place all ingredients in a jar and store in the fridge over night in the morning toss the ingredients in the blender and blend until smooth.

Healthy Chocolate flavored Smoothie

Serves 2
Nutritional Value: Calories: 451, Total Carbohydrates: 49.8g, Total Fats: 19.2g, Protein: 33.4g

Prep Time: 5 minutes

Ingredients
1 Oz lecithin
2 Oz sprinkle fiber
5 ice cubes
1 frozen banana
2 cups grain milk (gluten free)
2 scoops whey protein powder (chocolate flavored)

Instructions
Pour ingredients in blender and blend for around 45 seconds or until completely smooth.

Carrot Smoothie

Serves 1

Nutritional Value: Calories: 240, Total Carbohydrates: 8.0g, Total Fats: 4.0g, Protein: 42.0g

Prep Time: 5 minutes

Ingredients

1 Oz lecithin
1 Oz hemp oil
8 Oz natural carrot juice
2 scoops whey protein powder (vanilla flavored)

Instructions

Pour ingredients in blender and blend for around 45 seconds or until completely smooth.

Carrot Smoothie

Berry Smoothie

Serves 1
Nutritional Value: Calories: 360, Total Carbohydrates: 56.7g, Total Fats: 4.5g, Protein: 22.7g

Prep Time: 5 minutes

Ingredients

1 cup frozen berries
1 large banana
2 scoops protein powder
20 ounces of rice milk

Instructions

Pour ingredients in blender and blend for around 45 seconds or until completely smooth.

Berry Smoothie

Peach Smoothie

Serves 1
Nutritional Value: Calories: 151, Total Carbohydrates: 22g, Total Fats: 8g, Protein: 4g

Prep Time: minutes

Ingredients
2 teaspoon flax seed meal
1 tablespoon chopped walnuts
½ cup kale leaves
1/12 cup frozen peach slices
½ cup frozen banana slices
½ cup coconut milk

Instructions
Pour ingredients in blender and blend for around 45 seconds or until completely smooth.

Exotic Island Smoothie

Serves 1
Nutritional Value: Calories: 195, Total Carbohydrates: 41.8g, Total Fats: 2.2g, Protein: 3.4g

Prep Time: 5 minutes

Ingredients
2 teaspoon crushed coconut
¼ Oz flaxseed meal
1/8 cup dried plums
1 banana, peeled, frozen and sliced
½ an apple, chopped
½ cup water

Instructions
Pour ingredients in blender and blend for around 45 seconds or until completely smooth.

Summertime Smoothie

Serves 1

Nutritional Value: Calories: 258, Total Carbohydrates: 65.6g, Total Fats: 0.2g, Protein: 2.3g

Prep Time: 5 minutes

Ingredients

½ cup frozen strawberry slices
½ cup fresh mango diced
½ cup organic blueberries
½ cup peeled and frozen banana slices

Instructions

Pour ingredients in blender and blend for around 45 seconds or until completely smooth.

Citrus Smoothie

Serves 1
Nutritional Value: Calories: 94, Total Carbohydrates: 24.0g, Total Fats: 0.4g, Protein: 1.1g

Prep Time: 5 minutes

Ingredients

½ frozen and peeled bananas
½ cup blueberries, blackberries and raspberries
½ cup non diary milk (preferably unsweetened)

Instructions

Pour ingredients in blender and blend for around 45 seconds or until completely smooth.

Fruit Assortment Smoothie

Serves 1

Nutritional Value: Calories: 385, Total Carbohydrates: 25.9g, Total Fats: 31.4g, Protein: 5.2g

Prep Time: 5 minutes

Ingredients

2 teaspoons coconut flakes (unsweetened)
2 teaspoons flaxseed meal
¼ cup fresh blueberries
½ a banana
½ cup fresh mango chunks
½ cup coconut milk (unsweetened)

Instructions

Pour ingredients in blender and blend for around 45 seconds or until completely smooth.

Fruits and Veggies in One

Mixed Greens and Pecan Smoothie

Serves 1
Nutritional Value: Calories: 128, Total Carbohydrates: 22g, Total Fats: 6g, Protein: 2g

Prep Time: 5 minutes

Ingredients
½ Oz chopped pecans
¼ cup frozen raspberries
½ frozen bananas
½ cup mixed greens
½ cup water

Instructions
Pour ingredients in blender and blend for around 45 seconds or until completely smooth.

Banana and Spinach Smoothie

Serves 1
Nutritional Value: Calories: 239, Total Carbohydrates: 54.0g, Total Fats: 1.8g, Protein: 5.4g

Prep Time: 5 minutes

Ingredients
1 teaspoon spirulina powder
1 teaspoon kelp powder
2 teaspoons flaxseed meal
1 banana
½ cup spinach leaves
1 unpeeled Bosc pear
½ cup water

Instructions
Pour ingredients in blender and blend for around 45 seconds or until completely smooth.

Buttery and Citrus Banana Smoothie

Serves 2
Nutritional Value: Calories: 175, Total Carbohydrates: 17.3g, Total Fats: 8.3g, Protein: 9.9g

Prep Time: 5 minutes

Ingredients
Graham cracker bits (gluten free)
8 ice cubes
4 cups baby spinach (organic)
1 Oz sunflower butter
4 drops liquid stevia
½ teaspoon vanilla extract (pure)
1 frozen banana
2 cups non diary milk
2 teaspoons key lime zest
2 Oz key lime juice

Instructions
Pour ingredients in blender and blend for around 45 seconds.

Apple and Spinach Smoothie

Serves 2
Nutritional Value: Calories: 281, Total Carbohydrates: 43.2g, Total Fats: 10.4g, Protein: 6.1g

Prep Time: 5 minutes

Ingredients
Dash of salt
¼ teaspoon crushed cinnamon
½ teaspoon vanilla extract (pure)
4 pitted medjool dates
4 cups spinach
2 Oz sun butter
2 apples
2 cups unsweetened almond milk

Instructions
Pour ingredients in blender and blend for around 45 seconds.

Apple Juice Smoothie

Serves 1
Nutritional Value: Calories: 94, Total Carbohydrates: 12.0g, Total Fats: 3.1g, Protein: 6.1g

Prep Time: 1 hour

Ingredients
1 frozen banana (peeled and sliced)
½ cup sliced strawberries
3 medjool dates
1/8 cup apple juice (unsweetened)
1/8 cup soy milk
2 Oz tofu (extra firm)

Instructions
Soak the medjool dates in warm water 60 minutes prior to pouring all the ingredients in to the blender and pulsing until smooth.

Buttery Banana Smoothie

Serves 2

Nutritional Value: Calories: 320, Total Carbohydrates: 19.1g, Total Fats: 19.5g, Protein: 14.5g

Prep Time: 5 minutes

Ingredients

1 Oz almond butter (raw)
2 Oz flax seeds
1 frozen banana
8 ice cubes
4 cups spinach (organic)
2 cups almond milk (unsweetened)

Instructions

Pour all the ingredients in the food blender and blend till smooth.

Fruit and Vegan Smoothie

Serves 1
Nutritional Value: Calories: 133, Total Carbohydrates: 25g, Total Fats: 4g, Protein: 3g

Prep Time: 5 minutes

Ingredients
3 teaspoons flaxseed meal
1.2 cup mixed greens (fresh, whatever you choose)
½ cup strawberry slices
½ cup frozen banana slices
½ cup rice milk (unsweetened)

Instructions
Pour ingredients in blender and blend for around 45 seconds or until completely smooth.

Peachy Coconut Smoothie

Serves 2

Nutritional Value: Calories: 35, Total Carbohydrates: 8.4g, Total Fats: 0.2g, Protein: 0.9g

Prep Time: 5 minutes

Ingredients
½ cup peaches
½ cup grapes
1 cup coconut water
¾ cup fresh spinach

Instructions
Pour ingredients in blender and blend for around 45 seconds or until completely smooth.

Refreshing mango and Pineapple Smoothie

Serves 2
Nutritional Value: Calories: 149, Total Carbohydrates: 37.1g, Total Fats: 0.6g, Protein: 1.7g

Prep Time: 5 minutes

Ingredients

1 frozen and peeled banana
1 cup fresh mango, diced
½ cup pineapple slices
1 cup water
1 cup fresh spinach

Instructions

Pour ingredients in blender and blend for around 45 seconds or until completely smooth.

Orange and Berry Blend

Serves 2

Nutritional Value: Calories: 107, Total Carbohydrates: 26.4g, Total Fats: 0.5g, Protein: 1.8g

Prep Time: 5 minutes

Ingredients

1 peeled and frozen banana
½ cup blueberries
½ cup strawberries
1/3 cup natural orange juice
1/3 cup water
1 cup spinach

Instructions

Pour ingredients in blender and blend for around 45 seconds or until completely smooth.

Sweet Mango and Spinach Smoothie

Serves 2
Nutritional Value: Calories: 119, Total Carbohydrates: 17.6g, Total Fats: 3.3g, Protein: 5.4g

Prep Time: 5 minutes

Ingredients
1/3 cup avocado slices
½ cup pineapple slices
1 ½ cup water
¾ cup diced mango
¼ cup fresh cilantro
¾ cup fresh spinach

Instructions
Pour ingredients in blender and blend for around 45 seconds or until completely smooth.

Sweet Cinnamon and Cacao Smoothie

Serves 2
Nutritional Value: Calories: 381, Total Carbohydrates: 32.4g, Total Fats: 29.4g, Protein: 4.3g

Prep Time: 5 minutes

Ingredients

1 tablespoon cacao powder
Pinch of cinnamon
1 frozen and peeled banana
1 cup cherries
1 cup almond milk
1 cup spinach

Instructions

Pour ingredients in blender and blend for around 45 seconds or until completely smooth.

Berry and Spinach Smoothie

Serves 2
Nutritional Value: Calories: 287, Total Carbohydrates: 24.6g, Total Fats: 10.4g, Protein: 21.1g

Prep Time: 5 minutes

Ingredients
1 Dropper of liquid stevia
1 Oz frozen greens
1 scoop flavored protein powder
2 Oz ground flax seed
2 Oz slice d avocado
3 cups baby spinach
16 Oz coconut water
2 cups frozen blueberries

Instructions
Pour ingredients in blender and blend for around 45 seconds or until completely smooth.

Green Smoothie with a touch of Cacao and Citrus

Serves 4

Nutritional Value: Calories: 399, Total Carbohydrates: 18.6g, Total Fats: 34.9g, Protein: 9.9g

Prep Time: 5 minutes

Ingredients

6 ice cubes
1 Oz cacao powder
1 Oz coconut slices
2 Oz flax seed, crushed
2 cups raspberries
4 cups organic spinach
2 cups almond milk (unsweetened)

Instructions

Pour ingredients in blender and blend for around 45 seconds or until completely smooth.

Honey and Coconut Smoothie

Serves 5
Nutritional Value: Calories: 372, Total Carbohydrates: 21.1g, Total Fats: 33.1g, Protein: 5.3g

Prep Time: 5 minutes

Ingredients
8 ice cubes
2 cups frozen berries
2 teaspoons spirulina
1 Oz honey
1 Oz coconut oil
1 Oz almond butter
1 Oz cacao powder
2 cups spinach
2 cups almond milk (unsweetened)

Instructions
Pour ingredients in blender and blend for around 45 seconds or until completely smooth.

Vanilla flavored Green Smoothie

Serves 2

Nutritional Value: Calories: 457, Total Carbohydrates: 24.5g, Total Fats: 35.4g, Protein: 14.7g

Prep Time: 5 minutes

Ingredients

6 ice cubes
1 Oz vanilla almond flax butter
1 frozen banana
1 avocado
4 cups spinach (preferably organic)
2 cups non diary milk (unsweetened)

Instructions

Pour ingredients in blender and blend for around 45 seconds.

Breakfast Smoothies

Peanut butter and Oatmeal Smoothie

Serves 1

Nutritional Value: Calories: 100, Total Carbohydrates: 3.0g, Total Fats: 8.0g, Protein: 5.0g

Prep Time: 5 minutes

Ingredients

½ cup of chocolate light silk
½ package of instant oatmeal
½ of a frozen banana
1 tablespoon natural peanut butter

Instructions

Add the oatmeal into ¼ cup of boiling water and wait for a couple of minutes. Pour ingredients in blender and blend for around 45 seconds or until completely smooth.

Banana and Berry for Breakfast

Serves 2
Nutritional Value: Calories: 179, Total Carbohydrates: 28.5g, Total Fats: 3.7g, Protein: 7.0g

Prep Time: 5 minutes

Ingredients
½ cup ice cubes
1 cup frozen berries (whatever you choose)
2 peeled and frozen bananas
¾ cup soy milk

Instructions
Pour ingredients in blender and blend for around 45 seconds or until completely smooth.

Orange Smoothie

Serves 1
Nutritional Value: Calories: 240, Total Carbohydrates: 8.0g, Total Fats: 4.0g, Protein: 42.0g

Prep Time: 5 minutes

Ingredients
½ cup plain kefir
4 ice cubes
2 cups water
2 peeled oranges
2 scoops whey protein powder (vanilla flavor)

Instructions
Pour ingredients in blender and blend for around 45 seconds or until completely smooth.

Almond Meal Smoothie

Serves 1

Nutritional Value: Calories: 128, Total Carbohydrates: 27.7g, Total Fats: 2.0g, Protein: 2.0g

Prep Time: 5 minutes

Ingredients

2 teaspoon almond meal
¼ cup pitted and frozen cherries
1 banana
1 cup water

Instructions

Pour ingredients in blender and blend for around 45 seconds or until completely smooth.

Almond Meal Smoothie

Avocado and Cucumber Smoothie

Serves 2
Nutritional Value: Calories: 130, Total Carbohydrates: 10.1g, Total Fats: 8.9g, Protein: 6.0g

Prep Time: 5 minutes

Ingredients

1 cup water
7 ice cubes
½ frozen avocado, diced
4 cups spinach
1 English cucumber
Dash of crushed nutmeg
½ teaspoon vanilla extract
1 teaspoon crushed cinnamon
1 Oz walnuts
1 cup natural unsweetened apple juice

Instructions

If you cannot find vanilla extract you can use maple extract as a substitute. Place all ingredients into the blender and blend for 45 seconds.

The Perfect Breakfast Smoothie

Serves 2

Nutritional Value: Calories: 409, Total Carbohydrates: 67.0g, Total Fats: 12.8g, Protein: 9.8g

Prep Time: 5 minutes (prepare ingredients overnight)

Ingredients
Dash of crushed cinnamon
1 Oz walnuts
1 teaspoon vanilla extract
2 Cups al almond milk (preferably unsweetened)
1 Oz raisins
2 Oz oats
2 bananas

Instructions
Place all ingredients in a jar and store in the fridge over night in the morning toss the ingredients in the blender and blend until smooth.

Cinnamon Sweet Smoothie

Serves 1

Nutritional Value: Calories: 220, Total Carbohydrates: 45.5g, Total Fats: 2.9g, Protein: 6.2g

Prep Time: 5 minutes

Ingredients
Pinch of nutmeg
1.2 teaspoon ground cinnamon
1 frozen banana
1/8 cup date honey
¼ cup rice milk
3 Oz silken tofu

Instructions
Pour ingredients in blender and blend for around 45 seconds or until completely smooth.

Strawberry and Medjool Smoothie

Serves 1

Nutritional Value: Calories: 406, Total Carbohydrates: 40.2g, Total Fats: 29.0g, Protein: 3.8g

Prep Time: 5 minutes

Ingredients

1 medjool date
½ cup frozen strawberries
3 frozen strawberries
1 frozen banana
½ cup almond milk

Instructions

Pour ingredients in blender and blend for around 45 seconds or until completely smooth.

Plain Strawberry, Banana Smoothie

Serves 2
Nutritional Value: Calories: 203, Total Carbohydrates: 39.3g, Total Fats: 6.2g, Protein: 2.5g

Prep Time: 5 minutes

Ingredients

2 frozen bananas
2 cups strawberries
3 tablespoons of almond milk (unsweetened preferred)

Instructions

Pour ingredients in blender and blend for around 45 seconds or until completely smooth.

Natural Peanut Butter and Banana Smoothie

Serves 2
Nutritional Value: Calories: 83, Total Carbohydrates: 2.8g, Total Fats: 7.1g, Protein: 3.5g

Prep Time: 5 minutes

Ingredients
4 frozen bananas
1 Oz peanut butter (natural)
4-6 ice cubes

Instructions
Pour ingredients in blender and blend for around 45 seconds or until completely smooth.

Natural Peanut Butter and Strawberry Smoothie

Serves 2
Nutritional Value: Calories: 227, Total Carbohydrates: 24.0g, Total Fats: 14.3g, Protein: 4.2g

Prep Time: 5 minutes

Ingredients
4 tablespoons almond milk (unsweetened)
1 Oz peanut butter (natural)
3 cups frozen strawberries

Instructions
Pour ingredients in blender and blend for around 45 seconds or until completely smooth.

Fresh Mango Smoothie

Serves 2

Nutritional Value: Calories: 69, Total Carbohydrates: 17.6g, Total Fats: 0.6g, Protein: 0.6g

Prep Time: 5 minutes

Ingredients

2 Oz plain almond milk (preferably unsweetened)
1 ½ fresh mango, diced

Instructions

Pour ingredients in blender and blend for around 45 seconds or until completely smooth.

Citrus and Peach Smoothie

Serves 2

Nutritional Value: Calories: 70, Total Carbohydrates: 17.2g, Total Fats: 0.1g, Protein: 1.0g

Prep Time: 5 minutes

Ingredients

1 cup frozen pineapple slices
½ cup frozen peaches
½ cup frozen strawberries
1 peeled and frozen banana
1 Oz orange juice concentrate (frozen)

Instructions

Pour ingredients in blender and blend for around 45 seconds or until completely smooth.

Berry Smoothie

Serves 2

Nutritional Value: Calories: 211, Total Carbohydrates: 43.2g, Total Fats: 2.8g, Protein: 5.5g

Prep Time: 5 minutes

Ingredients

1 cup fresh berries
2 peeled and frozen bananas
1 cup soy milk

Instructions

Pour ingredients in blender and blend for around 45 seconds or until completely smooth.

Butter and Banana Smoothie

Serves 2

Nutritional Value: Calories: 365, Total Carbohydrates: 64.3g, Total Fats: 10.0g, Protein: 10.4g

Prep Time: 5 minutes

Ingredients

1 cup soy milk
1 Oz natural peanut butter
4 peeled and frozen ripe bananas

Instructions

Pour ingredients in blender and blend for around 45 seconds or until completely smooth.

Smoothies Rich in Antioxidants

Green Tea Smoothie

Serves 2
Nutritional Value: Calories: 191, Total Carbohydrates: 45.3g, Total Fats: 1.4g, Protein: 6.2g

Prep Time: 5 minute

Ingredients
1 inch ginger root
2 teaspoon freshly squeezed lemon juice
2 cups organic green tea
4 cups honeydew melon, diced
6 cups raw spinach
2 sliced cucumbers

Instructions
Blend all ingredients until smooth.

Fruit, veggie and Peppermint Smoothie

Serves 2

Nutritional Value: Calories: 179, Total Carbohydrates: 41.5g, Total Fats: 1.2g, Protein: 3.1g

Prep Time: 35 minutes

Ingredients

3 Oz non diary chocolate chips
10 ice cubes
2 Oz hemp hearts
2 bananas
4 cups spinach
1 cup rice milk
2 teabags of peppermint
1 cup boiled water

Instructions

Steep the teabags in the hot water for around half an hour. Reserve the chocolate chips and place the rest of the ingredients in the blender (including the peppermint tea solution). Blend until smooth. Drop half of the chocolate chips in the blender and pulse the machine quickly one last time. Before serving top each smoothie cup with the non blended chocolate chips.

Simple Herbal tea Smoothie

Serves 2
Nutritional Value: Calories: 224, Total Carbohydrates: 30.1g, Total Fats: 2.6g, Protein: 22.6g

Prep Time: 5 minutes (prepare ingredients overnight)

Ingredients
2 scoops protein powder
2 cups green teas or herbal tea
2 cup blueberries
1 peach

Instructions
Place all ingredients in a jar and store in the fridge over night in the morning toss the ingredients in the blender and blend until smooth.

Made in the USA
Lexington, KY
29 July 2016